40 Days With Faith

A Devotional for women who seek God's healing

Constance Ridley Smith

authorHOUSE'

AuthorHouse™
1663 Liberty Drive
Bloomington, IN 47403
www.authorhouse.com
Phone: 833-262-8899

Published by AuthorHouse 10/09/2020

ISBN: 978-1-4670-6239-8 (sc)
ISBN: 978-1-4670-6238-1 (e)

*H*ealing comes by faith.

The journey through illness is a faith walk. When that journey leads to a complete restoration of physical health, we are pleased. When it leads a person to salvation, God is pleased. In some cases, the journey leads to both.

In this devotional, we will:
- examine the role of faith in the healing process
- explore the cause of disease and illness
- discuss the healing power that resides in the Lord's Goodness, Virtue, Love, and Touch
- examine Five Traits shared by those who were healed by Christ
- show how women and men of faith displayed these traits as they sought healing, and
- discover what they did as a result of receiving healing.

The Five Traits of those who were healed are Faith … Humility … Importunity … Obedience … Ministry

DAY 1

Women of Faith Journey to Wellness

Faith is total reliance upon God. It is based on tenacious conviction and belief in God. Despite evidence to the contrary or what appears on the surface, a Christian woman of faith believes in the power of God to accomplish *His will* on earth. When a woman's will is aligned with the will of God, she can watch Him do the impossible on her behalf.

Faith, therefore, is more about a woman bringing her will into harmony with God's will than it is an exercise whereby she can cajole and convince God to do something other than His perfect will. The Lord's Prayer sums it up quite nicely, "Thy will be done on earth, as it is in Heaven." (Matthew 6:10).

The Bible discusses faith from many points of reference. We remember Peter's lack of faith when he tried to walk on water as Christ had done. Through his lacking, we understand that our faith will fail when we depend on our own strength and take our eyes off of the Master.

Faith can be readily understood by reflecting upon the ministry of Christ as he healed and restored men and women of the Bible. Because of their belief in Him, they experienced the outpour of His goodness, His virtue, His love; and they were healed. In the healing process, each person who was healed by Christ demonstrated five traits: faith, humility, importunity, and obedience. Their response to Him was ministry.

While the primary focus of this devotional will be the women who were healed by Jesus, these five traits—Faith, Humility, Importunity, Obedience, and Ministry—were found in those who were healed, men and women, alike.

You will read about a woman whose strength was restored and others who were delivered from demons and infirmities, which included a curved spine, an issue of blood, high fever, and an unclean spirit. One woman was even raised from the dead. These accounts are found in the Gospels of Mathew, Mark, Luke and John. We will make reference to all four of these books of the Bible in our discussion because sometimes one writer of the Gospel has included information or given a perspective that is not found in the other three books.

What miracle are you trusting God to perform in your life?

Be sure to know that:

"God is our refuge and strength, a very present help in trouble."
Psalm 46:1

DAY 2

All four of the Gospels (Matthew, Mark, Luke, and John) are intriguing. However, it is the book attributed to Luke that helps us to recognize all the branches of medicine that Jesus practiced. In some circles, Luke is commonly referred to as the New Testament physician. The book of Luke is like a medical journal found in the Bible between the books of Mark and John. The following outline of the book of Luke will show the branches of medicine that Jesus practiced. This outline may also become helpful when you want to cross-reference these stories of healing later, in your own studies. Read through His credentials. Can you trust Him to manage your health condition?

Here is a quick overview of Luke's "medical journal," describing the medical practice of Jesus Christ.

Chapter 1—gynecology and obstetrics; Luke tells about the pregnancies of Elisabeth and Mary

Chapter 2—pediatrics; neonatal and pediatric care of the young Christ child

Chapter 3—gerontology; genealogy of Christ

Chapters 4 and 6—family medicine; general healings of those who were ill

Chapters 5 and 6—Leprosy, palsy, dropsy, foaming at the mouth, crying out, plagues, demon possession and blindness were cured in these chapters.

Chapter 7—tells of a centurion's servant who was healed from "near death."

Chapter 8—mentions Mary Magdalene, a forgiven woman, who was healed of seven diseases; it also mentions Joanna, Susanna and many other women who were healed. Chapter 8 also notes how a woman's 12-year menstrual flow was stopped; it ends with Jairus' daughter who was raised from her deathbed.

Chapter 9—dietetics—nutritional needs were met as Christ fed the five thousand

Chapter 10—wellness; Christ gave lessons on stress management to Martha

Chapter 11—psychiatry and mental health; Christ cast out devils

Chapter 13—orthopedics and neurology were balanced by psychiatry in Chapter 13, as Jesus cured the woman in the bowed down condition.

Chapters 17 and 18—dermatology and ophthalmology; the ten lepers were cured of their skin condition and a blind man's vision was restored.

In another gospel, Jesus compounded and dispensed his own medicines (pharmacology). Read John 9:6. What a clinic! When Jesus showed up, healing took place.

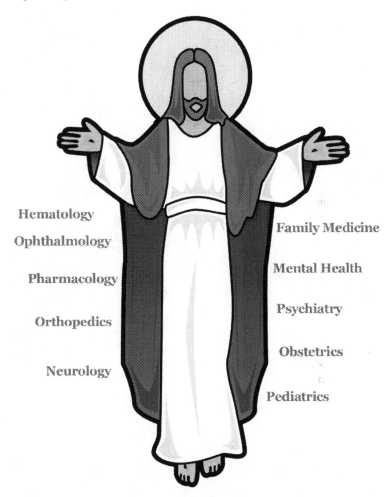

Hematology

Ophthalmology

Pharmacology

Orthopedics

Neurology

Family Medicine

Mental Health

Psychiatry

Obstetrics

Pediatrics

In addition to the women that Luke named, we find several other women (and men) who were cured by Jesus. Both Matthew and Mark wrote about Simon Peter's mother-in-law who was cured of a high fever and the daughter of a Gentile woman who was rid of an unclean spirit.

The condition and the healing process of each of those who were healed by Christ has been my source of inspiration and guidance. Because of their stories, I know that you and I can claim the healing and delivering power of Jesus Christ. Our response must be ministry.

You are not alone in your illness. It is also quite possible that you found your malady listed in Dr. Luke's Medical Journal on pages 4 and 5. Just know that the Christ of healing is the same today, yesterday, and forevermore. You can count on Him.

"Bless the Lord, O my soul, and forget not all his benefits: Who forgiveth all thine iniquities; who healeth all thy diseases…"

Psalm 103: 2-4

DAY 3

What caused their diseases?

We have mentioned Mary Magdalene, Simon Peter's mother-in-law, Jairus' daughter, the daughter of a Gentile woman, the woman with the issue of blood, and another woman who had a curvature of the spine. Each of these sick women either suffered from a lack of strength, or they were afflicted by a demon or an unclean (evil) spirit. From my study, I have concluded that both of these causes of infirmity are basically the same as modern-day diseases. In fact, the two English language words, infirmity and disease, are derived from the same Greek word, "asthenia."

Chart 1 below illustrates this.

The GREEK WORD Asthenia is the same as…	The ENGLISH WORDS lack of strength …	And the ENGLISH WORD… Disease
Asthenia= (Sthenos)=	Lack of strength= (Strength)=	Disease (Health)
Comment: In Vine's Expository Dictionary, the word infirmity is said to be the Greek asthenia, which literally means "lack of strength" as opposed to sthenos, which means strength. As such, the Bible promise of II Corinthians 12:9 takes on a deeper meaning, when applied to our health conditions… in His sthenos, we see our asthenia, not just our weakness, but our condition, caused by our lack of strength. That is, our illness or disease.		

The Bible confirms that we will not always have the strength of our youth, so we must do our best to keep our bodies fit and functioning well. Pray for strength and courage to embrace your body as it changes. Pray also for a sound mind. If illness comes upon you, seek Christ in prayer.

"The days of our years are threescore years and ten; and if by reason of strength they be fourscore years, yet is their strength labour and sorrow; for it is soon cut off, and we fly away."

Psalm 90:10

DAY 4

Can disease be caused by an unclean spirit?

When I was a teacher, students always complained about having to take algebra. They would ask, "Why do I need to take algebra anyway? How will algebra help me in my everyday life?" Or, "When am I going to use this in real life?" they would complain.

Today we're going to use the logic of algebra to figure out the relationships between diseases and their probable causes.

In algebra, there is a formula that states:

If $a=b$

And $b=c$,

Then $a=c$

Using this logic:
If unclean spirits are sometimes demonic in nature,

And demons cause diseases,

Then there is a relationship between demonic, unclean spirits and diseases.

Algebraic logic can also be applied, as follows:

If asthenia is a word used for illness,

And asthenia simply means a lack of strength,

then some illnesses are simply caused by a lack of strength that is related to some body part or body system that is not functioning up to par.

Both unclean spirits and demons negatively affect health and well-being. Both cause infirmity. Both cause illnesses. One way to combat the battle for your mental stability is to fix your thoughts on positive things. Paul's letter to the believers in Phillipi sums it up perfectly,

"Finally, brethren, whatsoever things are true, whatsoever things are honest, whatsoever things are just, whatsoever things are pure, whatsoever things are lovely, whatsoever things are of good report; if there be any virtue, and if there be any praise, think on these things."

Phillipians 4:8

DAY 5

Scripture describes the Gentile Woman (also called Canaanite/Greek/Syrophoenician) whose daughter had an unclean spirit. The woman sought healing for her daughter. Her actions show us how important it is to intercede on behalf of others and petition for their healing. What a symbol of caring and affinity—to passionately seek the healing of another person. Often persons who are very ill cannot pray for themselves. One woman who suffered as she was battling cancer confided in me, "I was too sick to pray." To know that your intercession can be a blessing in someone else's life is unmatched privilege.

This text uses the word "spirit" with a lowercase "s" (See Mark 7:25). In the Greek language, this "spirit" is the word, "pneuma." A look in the *Expository Dictionary of Biblical Terms* shows that the word used in this scripture is the Greek word, daimonion, the same Greek word used for demon. Refer to Chart 2 as you consider these facts about daimonion or demons:

Chart 2 below illustrates this.

The GREEK WORD Daimonion is the same as…	The ENGLISH WORD Demon	And the ENGLISH WORD "spirit," written in the Bible with the lowercase "s".
Daimonion	Demon	(evil) spirit
Comment: When the Bible refers to the type of spirit that causes diseases, "spirit" is often preceded by the word, words "evil" or "unclean" and, typically, is written with a lower-case "s.". It is typically a translation of the Greek word, daimonion.		

Because the Greek word for Holy Spirit and Spirit of Truth is also *pneuma*, and is often written with a lowercase "s", we have to determine the use of *pneuma* through the contextual clues from each passage of scripture. It is important to note that every "pneuma" is not controlled by a daimonion, however, the next verse in the passage of scripture (Mark 7:26) confirms that this unclean spirit was a devil. When referring to type of spirit that produces negative consequences like illness, spirit is always lowercase and is usually preceded by the word, unclean.

Today, you may be suffering physically, mentally, or emotionally. You may be weak in the body and lack physical strength. Or you may feel that your mind has been attacked by the power of unclean spirits and unholy thoughts. You can pray to God to watch over you, bless your family, and keep your mind clear. Rest, knowing this Bible promise is true:

"He giveth power to the faint; and to them that have no might he increaseth strength."

Isaiah 40:29

DAY 6

An unclean spirit (daimonion) can affect either the body or the mind with conditions of disease:

> And I saw three unclean spirits like frogs, out of the mouth of the Dragon and out of the mouth of the beast and out of the mouth of the false prophet for they are the spirits of devils …

An unclean spirit (akarthartos) can affect the body and the mind with conditions of disease:

> For a certain woman whose young daughter had an unclean spirit heard of Him and came and fell at His feet (Mark 7:25).

> While Jesus was preaching in a synagogue, and behold there was a woman which had a spirit of infirmity 18 years, and was bowed together, and could in no wise lift up herself (Luke 13:11).

A spirit of infirmity (asthenia) can cause weakness in the body.
In scripture, the words evil spirit and infirmities are often paired together:

> And certain women, which had been healed of evil spirits and infirmities, Mary called Magdalene, out of whom went seven devils … (Luke 8:2)

> While Jesus was preaching in a synagogue, and behold there was a woman who had a spirit of infirmity 18 years, and was bowed together, and could in no wise lift up herself. (Luke 13:11)

Luke 13:11 explains that while Jesus was preaching in a synagogue, a woman who had a spirit of infirmity came in. Her body was in a bowed down condition. She had been in this condition for eighteen years. The Bible describes the woman as a daughter of Abraham (Luke 13: 16), a term used for a woman who was a believer. This suggests that there may be women in our churches who have the same conditions, ailments and issues as women outside the church. It affirms that illness can affect a woman's quality of life, without respect to her religious affiliation. The only difference between the two is how God's woman will react to the diagnosis and what her journey will look like from day to day.

Vine's Expository Dictionary goes on to say that the bowed down condition, in a modern way of looking at it, was a curvature of the spine. Dr. Luke's diagnosis showed no physical reason behind the curvature.

In fact, he called it a "spirit of infirmity," meaning being caused by a spirit. The spirit was of Satan (verse 16) and apparently affected the woman's mental, spiritual or emotional outlook, causing her to be bowed over. Some translations call the spirit a demon.

It is only through the Light of the World that we can discern the spiritual aspect of a condition or infirmity. In Christ's perfection we see our imperfection. In the Prince of Peace we notice our lack of peace. In His strength, we see our brokenness.

Lord, bless our minds that they may be healthy. Claim the promise:

"My grace is sufficient for thee for my strength
is made perfect in weakness."

I Corinthians 12:9

"For we wrestle not against flesh and blood, but against
principalities, against powers, against the rulers of the darkness
of this world, against spiritual wickedness in high places."

Ephesians 6:12

DAY 7

Vine's Expository Dictionary of Biblical Words concludes that this correlation of the women's infirmity with a spirit could have only been written by someone who was qualified as a medical practitioner. Vine's statement supports the opinion that Luke was indeed a physician.

When debilitating illness comes upon us we, like this woman, will not be able to do anything to rise above the condition ourselves (Read Luke 13:11). Our deliverance will be accomplished only by our faith in a Power greater than our own.

The inability to help oneself was also the condition of the woman who had an issue of blood for twelve years.

The Book of Mark states:
And a certain woman had an issue of blood for 12 years and had suffered many things of many physicians and had spent all that she had and had nothing bettered but rather grew worse (Mark 5: 25-26).

The Book of Luke records the same story:
And a woman having an issue of blood 12 years, which had spent all her living upon physicians, neither could be healed of any, came behind Him and touched the border of His garment: and immediately her issue of blood stanched (Luke 8: 43-44).

A blood flow stopped immediately from a touch? Can this be? This woman had, no doubt, been touched by the many physicians she had visited. Why was she not healed at any other point along the way? Why this touch?

It was the touch propelled by her faith that made the difference.

The woman, like others who were healed by Christ, had <u>faith</u> in His ability to heal. That's why Christ responded as he did :

To the woman with the issue of blood – "Daughter thy <u>faith</u> has made thee whole." (Mark 5:34)

To the Gentile woman whose daughter had an unclean spirit – "O woman, great is thy <u>faith</u>…" (Matthew 15:28)

To the two blind men – "According to thy <u>faith</u>, be it unto you…" (Matthew 9:28), and

To the Centurion's servant – "I have not found so great <u>faith</u>, no not in Israel…" (Matthew 8: 10)

My prayer is that your faith will increase. Put your trust in Jesus Christ, the Master Physician. Then select an earthly physician in whom you can also trust. Pray for a physician who is well-trained in understanding the workings of human body; who will seek the wisdom of God when he doesn't understand, and who will become empowered by the Almighty God to restore your health.

"Now faith is the substance of things hoped
for, the evidence of things not seen."

Hebrews 11:1

DAY 8

Goodness and Virtue. These are two words that describe the character of Christ with respect to His ability to heal by mere touch.

Luke Chapter 6 opens with several scenarios that reveal the character of Christ. Knowing His character is key to understanding the power of His touch. In Christ, there is goodness. He has power against the illnesses that are caused by evil spirits, because He is good. In short, the antidote for evil spirits caused by Satan is to seek the goodness of our Lord and Saviour. In Christ, there is also virtue. Before we discuss how to seek the goodness and virtue of Christ, let us probe Luke Chapter 6 to understand these character keys of Christ, with respect to healing. What motivated Christ to heal? What motivated people to seek Him for healing?

Luke 6 is written to show us what motivated Christ. Then, as it is now, Christ's primary motive was to do good in the lives of others. In Luke 6, Christ had been criticized by allowing his disciples to pluck and eat corn on the Sabbath day. On another Sabbath Day, Christ healed a man's withered hand. His response to the critics (the scribes and the Pharisees) is key to understanding His motive. He asked them, "Is it lawful on the Sabbath days to do good, or to do evil? To save life, or to destroy it?"

Christ wanted to save lives. This was evident to those around him. His motive to "do good" drew people to him. We know this because further in the same chapter, Christ went into a mountain to pray all night. After he came down from the mountain, He and His disciples stood in an open spot of land, a plain. A great multitude of people came to the plain. They came from Judea, Jerusalem, Tyre, and Sidon to hear Him and be healed of their diseases.

The second reason why the touch of Christ was a healing touch was due to his virtue. This is revealed in verse 19:

" ... came to hear him and be healed of their diseases; And

they that were vexed with unclean spirits: and they were healed. And the whole multitude sought to touch him: for there went virtue out of him, and healed them all."

If you are seeking to be healed, you have done the right thing. Seeking Christ is the wisest move that you've made.

"O God, Thou art my God; early will I seek Thee."

Psalm 63:1

DAY 9

Likewise, when the woman with the issue of blood touched the hem of His garment, His virtue went out of Him and healed her. The remedy for the evil spirits that Satan sends to create illness in our minds, our emotions and, consequently, our bodies is to pray and seek to come into the presence of His virtue. In order to be healed of daimonion and evil spirits, we must seek Christ. Although we can no longer physically touch Him or His garments, we can come apart, commune, pray, and meditate daily, hourly, or each minute of the day, as it is necessary, ask Him for strength to overcome. Healing comes as we call upon Him to help us to overcome the evil spirits that bind us. Our healing may not be immediate, but each call to Christ is like a dose of Divine medicine. It builds our connection to Him as the Healer and creates an exchange that will, in fact, bring us healing and victory over the evil spirits that bind us in illness and emotional distress.

In this life many things can happen to us. Sometimes we are exposed to the power of evil messages or spirits by what we see; the trauma or losses that we experience; gruesome events that we witness; how people treat us in relationships; or information that we come in contact with. In this century, information is literally exploding into our homes and into our personal space—by way of television, the Internet, music, and people that Satan employs as his agents. Sometimes these messages produce compulsive behaviors, addictions, and haunting images within our minds that can control or debilitate us and the ones we love. Our response to these messages can even make us physically ill. The antidote is to seek goodness and the virtue of Christ.

Go to a quiet place - a cabin in the mountains, a cottage by the sea, a sanitarium or wellness facility, if you can afford it. Remove yourself from the toxic environment and people who cause you emotional harm. The barest furniture, fewest articles of clothing, limited amounts of outside media for a period of time can work wonders for helping to restore your connection to His goodness and virtue.

If you cannot afford any of these retreats, find a hiking trail, a park, a special tree or a special place in nature where you can commune with God and feel the solitude that is necessary to bring healing. It is likely that one spot will become your favorite. Create a routine by selecting appointed times that you will visit your selected spot. Incorporate other rituals that are pleasing to you. When you reach that spot, you might open your thermos and enjoy a cool, refreshing drink of water from it.

Open your Bible or devotional and read a passage. Rehearse the Gems of Faith that are found on Day 28 of this devotional.

Whatever your economic means are, God is available to you to heal you and to restore your health and well-being.

"It is of the LORD's mercies that we are not consumed, because his compassions fail not. They are new every morning: great is thy faithfulness. The LORD is my portion, saith my soul; therefore will I hope in him."

Lamentations 3: 22-24

DAY 10

Love. Love is curative. Philosophers, authors, and songwriters agree that the human body's internal responses to hate, resentment, and unwillingness to forgive others can undermine one's own health and body functions. If that is the case, songwriter India Arie Simpson offers a simplistic, yet compelling prescription,

> *"The worst disease in the world is not cancer, it's not AIDS; The cure will not be found by any physicist or scientist; The cause and a cure live in every single one of us. The worst disease in the world is hate and the cure for hate is love. Oh Love, oh love, oh love…. the cure for hate is love."*
>
> (*The Cure*, India Arie Simpson)

Healing often comes from a loving "touch—by someone you love" and believe in and someone who you know loves and tenderly cares about you (Pearsall, 1987, p.262). In fact, that is why many health advisors tell those who are sick to "find a physician in whom you can believe." To that counsel, I might also add, "find one whose philosophy on life and dying matches your own."

Both women we have discussed, the one in the bowed down condition and the woman with the issue of blood, determined Christ to be such a physician. They had faith in His power to heal them. They accepted His demonstration of love for them. His love had the power to dispel their diseases. "What greater love hath any man than this?"

After I wrote the book, *Mothers of Faith*, upon which this devotional is based, I came to know a woman who suffered from a skin condition, like eczema. She told me that for several years she was in a scratch-itch cycle, scratching so much until her skin was raw and would often bleed. Like the woman with the issue of blood she was also anemic, but she could not stop the scratch-itch ritual. It controlled her life. She would get the urge to scratch and would not stop until it bled. It was unsightly and all who saw this area of her skin were mortified.

The young woman went from doctor to doctor, spending all she had (in a sense) on office visits, biopsies, labs, blood tests. There was no physical reason for her skin condition. It was not bacterial, viral, pathogenic, nor contagious. The last physician she visited told the woman, "The cause of this thing is not known." Another physician queried the woman, "What is bothering you?" The woman began to recall a litany of pressures caused by the cares of life, debt, trauma, bad relationships, abuse, death of loved ones and an encounter of a sexual nature that made her feel dirty and ashamed. She withdrew from all intimacy and literally began to hate the perpetrators of her abuse.

One evening in a retreat setting, she experienced the turning point in her recovery. As the group was in a prayer circle, holding hands, she began to feel, for the first time in a very long time, the love of God and its transforming power. She described to me the uplifting feeling that helped her, in time, to overcome the hatred that had bound her for years. Every time she remembered the hatred, the abuse, the loss, the trauma, the shame, or the guilt, she replaced those images with the image of the warmth, brotherly love, acceptance, and kindness that she had experienced that night in the prayer circle.

Finally, she became convinced that she was capable of living a whole life, or was at least willing to try it. She removed herself from the toxic environment. Over a period of time, she sought God for healing and through counselling, reading, living in harmony with the laws of nature, and reducing her anxiety, she found relief.

Within a few months, she was able to reduce the compulsive scratching. Her outlook improved. The raw skin healed and her emotions began to follow suit. The young woman claimed the promise found in Psalms 147:3:

"He healeth the broken in heart, and bindeth up their wounds."

Psalm 147:3

DAY 11

Closeness. Healing is often attached to closeness, both physical and emotional. For example, when David was stricken with old age, they brought a young maid to lie next to him (I Kings 1:1-4). When the prophet Elijah was called upon to heal the widow's son, he laid his body on the body of the lad (II Kings 4:35). That is part of our human condition—the need for closeness. People fare better in the hospital and recuperating from surgery when they have family support. Others gain power over diseases and habits when they are affiliated with a support group.

The power of loving touch is key to healing, but it is also essential for wellness. I was on the worship committee for our church. Those in charge were trying to figure out a way to shorten the services, which had gotten quite lengthy. The worship leader's suggestion was to trim the time by eliminating the greeting. In this church the greeting is the period of time where the musicians play lively music and persons can leave their seats and greet and hug others in the congregation. One woman let us know that her aunt, an elderly woman who lives alone, came to church only for *that* segment of the service. In fact, after the greeting, she rarely returned to her seat. She most often left the service, continuing out the side door, into the parking lot. In other words she came to church for the hugs and "warm fuzzies" that she received during that portion of the service. One elderly gentleman also joked that this was the only time a young woman wearing nice perfume would smile at him and give him a hug.

These stories underscore the desire we all have for human touch. One of our local physicians stated that in hospital neonatal units, the babies who are cuddled and held, thrive; those who are fed and bathed only, without cuddling, fail to thrive (also Lachkar, 1998, p. 43). In these ways, we are no different from the woman with the issue of blood.

By faith, the woman with the issue of blood associated Christ with hope for her wellness and she was thereby, healed. According to the Bible story, when she grabbed the hem of His garment, she received healing.

Yet, the healing power was not in His garment, but in her belief in the loving, transforming power of Christ who wore the garment. It was a transaction that was created in her mind, her spirit, and her emotions. Her healing was created first in her thought life.

Similarly, we can win the battle over many of our ailments by rehearsing positive messages in our minds rather than negative ones. For this reason, I encourage you to seek love, rather than hate.

"A merry heart doeth good like a medicine, but
a broken spirit dries up the bones."

Proverbs 17:22

DAY 12

A lack of strength also causes disease. Sometimes, illness does come from a breakdown in one or more body systems. We are genetically predisposed to certain illnesses by virtue of our family history. In those cases, illness is not caused by a demon, but by a lack of strength or poor functioning within one's body systems. Our lifestyle choices, eating, and exercise habits also contribute. Prolonged stress and our outlook on life can make these conditions flourish.

In fact, he suggests that the immune system is controlled by one's self-talk. He explains that there are certain diseases which affect persons who are explosive "hot reactors" and there are other diseases which affect those who withdraw and who are defeatist in their attitudes. For the latter group, these diseases include "allergies, arthritis, infections, diabetes, multiple sclerosis, lupus, and cancer"(p. 126). Dr. Pearsall calls these individuals the "cold reactors."

Pray today that God will bless your selection of physicians and other caregivers and that they will be led by God on your behalf.

Surround yourself with those who love you and tenderly care for you.

"The effectual, fervent prayer of a righteous
man [or woman] availeth much."

James 5:16

DAY 13

Now let's talk about many women of the Bible who found their healing. Their stories underline for us what faith in God can do to relieve our suffering. It reminds us that a woman can be a churchgoer or, perhaps, even a member and still find herself crippled by disease. She may not be able to lift herself. She can return home each time as she left home—spiritually low. She can come to church 18 years with a "demon" on her back. She can bleed physically or emotionally for 12 years and see no sign of relief.

What made the difference for these women? How can a woman find healing and deliverance from the demons or spirits of infirmity that bind her mentally, physically, spiritually, or emotionally?

The healings performed by Christ are based on His goodness and virtue and the loving touch He rendered. But those that He healed demonstrated five common traits during their healing process. Those five traits are:

1. Humility
(a bowed down condition)
> The Bible illuminates: If my people, which are called by my name, shall humble themselves, and pray, and seek my face, and turn from their wicked ways; then will I hear from heaven, and will forgive their sin, and will heal their land. (II Chronicles 7:14)

2. Faith
(seeking the word of God or the Word of God)
> The Bible explains: "Faith comes by hearing and hearing by the word of God." (Romans 10:27)

3. Importunity[3]
> (doing whatever is necessary to gain healing: perseverance, persistence) (Luke 11:5-8)

DAY 15

This woman knew first-hand what Paul would later write in Romans Chapter 10 verse 17: "Faith comes by hearing and hearing by the word of God." Her venture to the synagogue that day would allow her to hear the word of God being read and also to see the Word of God (Jesus), in the flesh.

To fully understand her healing, one must first understand that the Sabbath was ordained as a memorial of the creation week. On it, God rested from His creative activity. On it, we can obtain rest from earthly activity and become rejuvenated for the week ahead. When the ruler of the synagogue saw the woman, he looked at her disdainfully. He saw another poor, wretched soul. When Christ, the ruler of the Sabbath, saw the same woman He saw an opportunity to allow someone else to enjoy the rest, rejuvenation, and renewal that is available to all, each week, on the Sabbath day. This woman courageously made her way to the House of delivery on the day of deliverance. He, being the Lord of deliverance, loosed her bond and glorified God. Hallelujah!

3. The Syrophoencian Woman Had Humility and Faith; She Demonstrated Importunity

Our third example of healing was the Gentile woman whose daughter had an unclean spirit within her. Perhaps her story is included in the Bible to illustrate the value of "doing whatever it takes to receive that which you seek" (importunity).

It is interesting to note that this woman was a nonbeliever—at least to the human eye. Jesus' words to her, that it was not suitable to take the children's bread and throw it away to the dogs, underscored the fact that He knew that she was a Gentile, and potentially, a nonbeliever. However, the fact that she received healing for her daughter shows that Jesus was not an elitist, prejudiced, nor a supremacist. Today, as in those days, His blessings of healing are available to all. He does not limit healing to those who believe in Him.

4. Obedience
(following God's plan for our health, our healing, and for our lives) (Acts 5:29)

5. Ministry
(going on God's errands)
The Bible explains: But I have prayed for thee, that thy faith fail not: and when thou art converted, strengthen thy brethren.
(Luke 22:32)

"Behold, he that keepeth Israel shall neither slumber nor sleep."
Psalm 121:4

DAY 14

In the pages that follow, we will look at three women of the Bible and gain an understanding of how they exhibited faith, humility, and importunity during their journey to wellness. After that, we will examine and more fully define the elements in each of the five traits.

1. The Woman with the Issue of Blood
    Had Faith and Demonstrated her Humility

The woman with the issue of blood came behind Christ and touched the hem of His garment, which means she must have been crouched to the ground. This bowed down condition was the correct position for the woman with the issue of blood to assume in order to receive her deliverance; it symbolized her humility. She was low financially, low emotionally, ghastly anemic, yet she was spiritually astute enough to know that if she could just grasp the hem of His priestly robe, she could signify to Him that she believed in His Lordship and His power. This act demonstrated her faith. In those days it was commonly known that in the hem, priestly robes were trimmed with a ribbon of blue. The ribbon of blue symbolized Jesus' royalty and Kingship. By grasping for the hem, she knew that she could communicate what she was too weak and low to communicate with words. In an exchange that transcended earthly ears and human understanding, she called Him Lord, my Maker, my Healer and my Redeemer.

2. The Woman with the Spine Curvature
    Was in a Bowed Down Condition (Humility) and
    Demonstrated

A similar dynamic occurred with the woman who had been living in a bowed down condition for 18 years. She was perpetually in the position of humility, a bowed down condition. By making it to the synagogue on the Sabbath day, she proclaimed Him to be Lord of the Sabbath, Lord of creation, and Lord of her deliverance. For the same Lord who preached in the synagogue on the Sabbath, was the same Lord who created her,

and could therefore, heal and deliver her. This thinking was based on her belief in the Word of God, in other words, her faith.

"Faith cometh by hearing, and hearing, by the word of God."

Romans 10:17

Perhaps you are a non-believer. Or, maybe you are a believer whose walk with Christ has missed a few paces. Can you still call on Christ to heal you? Certainly. The Bible reminds us,

"...for He makes His sun rise on the evil and on the good, and sends rain on the just and on the unjust."

Matthew 5:45

EXAMINING THE FIVE TRAITS OF THOSE WHO WERE HEALED

DAY 16

Point 1. "What does it mean to have faith?"

In the face of illness and disease, some people gain strength by reciting a mantra of faith each day. They make statements such as, "I am trusting God to heal me." Their belief is that by saying it, it will come to pass. They base such practice on the first clause of the Bible verse, Proverbs 18:21, "Death and life are in the power of the tongue: and they that love it shall eat the fruit thereof."

Sometimes, however, despite their "name-it-and-claim-it" philosophy, the disease takes its ravaging course and the person succumbs to their mortality (earthly death).

Or, a person may have a debilitating condition which has a poor prognosis (expectancy for improvement). Initially, the debilitating condition defies the odds and the sufferer shows some indications of miraculous improvement. But despite further echoes of faith, the condition does not continue to improve.

Does this indicate that the believer did not have enough faith? Or, like medicine after its shelf-life, did their faith lose its efficacy? In both instances, the believers exercised faith. But what went wrong?

Perhaps there is a difference between what God thinks of as faith, and what man thinks of as faith. In most cases, Jesus responded to the person who was ill by saying "it is done because of your faith," "thy faith has made thee whole," or "go and sin no more." However, the Pharisees criticized Him for mixing the healing of illnesses with the forgiveness of sins. "Who is he," they asked, "who has the power to forgive sins?"

The ill person is looking for wellness of the body; Christ is looking for salvation of the soul. The journey through illness is a faith walk. When that journey leads to a complete restoration of physical health, we

!

are happy. When it leads a person to salvation, and what Christ meant by "whole," God is happy. Sometimes the journey leads to both. Sometimes it does not. When it does not, our crowning act of faith must be in the perfect bodies we will have in the earth made new (read Revelation 21:4).

"Thou he slay me, yet will I serve him."

Job 13:15

DAY 17

Point 2. What is humility?

In order to be the propitiation for our sins, Christ had to be born as a human and live on Earth, among men. The Bible records that He was in all ways tempted as we are tempted today. His willingness to walk among us gave Him first-hand experience about the conditions that we find ourselves trying to manage and overcome. That is why He can minister on our behalf, show us mercy in time of need, and see us through our journey toward wellness.

"For we have not an high priest which cannot be touched with the feeling of our infirmities; but was in all points tempted like as we are, yet without sin." Hebrews 4:15

"He is despised and rejected of men; a man of sorrows, and acquainted with grief …" Hebrews 53:3

"He was oppressed and He was afflicted, Yet He did not open His mouth; Like a lamb that is led to slaughter, And like a sheep that is silent before its shearers, so He did not open His mouth." Isaiah 53:7 NASV

Likewise, without suffering, we cannot have affinity with Christ, nor can we be in touch with our fellow man. We can better minister to others when we have also shared challenges similar to the ones they face. Our association with the challenges that others face allows us to 'go on God's errands' among our fellow man and to do as Christ would have done.

"A merry heart maketh a cheerful countenance: but by sorrow of the heart the spirit is broken."

Proverbs 15:12-14

DAY 18

Point 3. What is importunity?

Another look at the healing journeys of these three women shows one other similarity. We have determined that all three of them demonstrated faith and humility. The third characteristic they shared was their importunity.

Importunity is putting oneself in the position to receive that which one is seeking. In the healing process, importunity is a relentless search for wellness. For the woman with the issue of blood, it meant going to doctor after doctor, literally spending all she had. For the woman who had the curvature of the spine for 18 years, it meant making her way to where Jesus would be on the Sabbath day, at whatever cost. For the Syrophencian or Gentile woman, importunity was reaching across cultural biases to get what was needed for her daughter. All three women put themselves in the position to receive the blessing of healing.

Importunity is explained in the Bible through the parable Christ gave to His disciples in Luke Chapter 11: 5-8. In this parable, Jesus tells about one friend who comes to the other friend at midnight seeking food. Christ states that the sleeping man would rise and get food for his friend, not because of friendship, but because of his friend's importunity.

Later on in his book, Luke cites another parable to elaborate upon the concept of importunity. In Chapter 18, Christ speaks of a widow who stood before a judge that neither feared God, nor regarded man. As a judge, he was therefore morally unqualified to do the job he was entrusted to do. Christ disqualified this judge based on these two key attributes that are necessary for the position. His illustration shows the effectiveness of the widow's importunity in getting what she sought from the judge. If the judge had feared or reverenced God, he would have avenged the woman of her enemy based on the law of the Ten Commandments. If he had regarded man, he would have avenged the woman based on the Two Great Commandments recorded in the book of Matthew Chapter 1.

But because he neither regarded man, nor feared God, the woman's importunity was the key. Luke 18: 5 summarizes in this way:

"Yet because this widow troubleth me, I will avenge her, lest by her continual coming she weary me. And shall not God avenge his own elect, which cry day and night unto Him, though He bear long with them?

I tell you that he will avenge them speedily. Nevertheless when the Son of man cometh, shall He find faith on earth?"

In summary, importunity can be defined as shameless persistence[3].

It suggests putting oneself in the position to receive because of the expectation to receive. Importunity implies the requestor's impotence and the grantor's potency. The requestor seizes the opportunity that is before him. For example, the hungry friend put himself at the door of a man with children, a man who was likely to have food in the house. The woman with the spirit of infirmity put herself in the synagogue where Jesus was going to preach. The woman with the issue of blood pressed her way in the crowd behind Jesus, just close enough to touch the border of His garment (Mark 5:27). Simon (and Andrew) petitioned the Lord about Simon's mother-in-law's fever when He came to Simon's house (Mark 1:30). When Jesus departed into the coasts of Tyre and Sidon, the Gentile woman followed Him to ask for healing for her daughter (Matthew 15:21-22). The women healed of evil spirits and infirmity in Luke 8:2 got to Jesus by pressing their way to Him when He came into their midst. This is importunity.

"But they that wait upon the LORD shall renew their strength;
they shall mount up with wings as eagles; they shall run,
and not be weary; and they shall walk, and not faint."

Isaiah 40: 31

DAY 19

Point 4. Obedience

The fourth point of commonality among those who were healed is their obedience. Obedience is trapped in a foible of human nature. We cleverly rationalize against the simplicity of God's health counsel, for example, those which relate to diet, exercise, and the management of stress. And when we do decide to make changes in our lives, we often make them too late to bring a significant impact on our quality of life and, often, our mortality. We pass the paper/pencil test, but fail the application exercise. Like many, I have scoffed at natural remedies and God's simple plan for healthful living or restoring my health. I've selected the counsel that I believed to be important and rejected the other. I've often gained knowledge that I didn't incorporate into a lifestyle change. I now conclude that there is no remedy that will help without obedience to the recommended plan. It is not enough to hear and understand. We must apply that knowledge; this is the essence of obedience.

Naaman the leper is a Biblical example which shows the power that is available when we, in obedience, follow the health counsel that has been given to us. Naaman was a highly credentialed man, but he was a leper. His skin condition (leprosy) was a physical illness, but according to Biblical principles, leprosy also indicated a spiritual lacking in Naaman's life. (You may recall that Moses' sister Miriam was also plagued with leprosy as a result of her unwillingness to accept Zipporah as Moses' wife).

The remedy that was spoken to Naaman through the prophet Elijah seemed to be a bit extreme. Namaan could not understand the significance of dipping his body into the Jordan River seven times. But it was only upon his full obedience to the prophet's plan that his skin condition was healed.

Whether the counsel is to reduce your consumption of sugar, starches and fried foods; add more fiber to your diet; adhere to a daily exercise routine; or make time for prayer, meditation, and relaxation, it is only through obedience to the counsel given that the struggle to regain our health can be won. God's plan wins out over man's.

What is God's plan for our health? What blessings will obedience to God's plan avail for our longevity and our quality of life? Does adherence to God's plan really matter?

Isaiah Chapter 58 contrasts the difference between God's perception and man's. From this passage of scripture, we can deduce that following God's plan is best.

To this I offer you, the reader, the same counsel that Paul offered to the members of the early church:

"We ought to obey God rather than men."

Acts 5:29

DAY 20

The main theme of Isaiah 58 is God's desire to save his people by pointing out their shortcomings, giving them a plan to achieve oneness with Him, and restoring them to their original purpose—to ride upon the "high places" of life. That is the definition of health. That is good living. And incidentally, that is what we also aspire to today.

The illustration used in Isaiah 58 centers on the concept of fasting. When we fast for healing, my impression and my experience has been that fasting removes the interference from unhealthy signals so that the body can regulate itself and/or benefit from treatment that is being given to restore one's health.

Fasting breaks the connection between the person and the offensive habit, practice, food, substance, thoughts, or thought patterns. In the absence of interference, the body can, many times, regulate itself. Fasting is an alignment activity. It's greatest value may not be in the denial of food or substance, but in the opportunity it provides to restore clear thinking.

But Isaiah 58 is much more than a commentary on the practice of fasting and denying oneself food and drink. The significance of the scripture is that it draws a contrast between what man thinks is appropriate and what God thinks is appropriate. It thereby serves as a guidepost for seeking God's will and obeying it, even in matters related to our health.

At the opening of chapter 58, God asks Isaiah to lift up his voice like a trumpet and show the Israelites (House of Jacob) their sins and transgressions. Through the prophet, they were instructed that their version of fasting was basically inadequate because it served their own purposes and self-directed motives. It didn't make a difference in the way they treated others. Violence and strife were still a part of their lives. In other words, their fast was full of form, but it did not contain substance. To those looking on, it appeared that they were reaching God. But God's counsel was clear,

"Ye shall not fast as ye do this day to make your voice to be heard on high." (Isaiah 58:4)

In verse 5 God asks them a question: "Is it such a fast that I have chosen?" God further explains that His own fast is one that looses the bands of wickedness, feeds the hungry, and ministers to the poor and less fortunate. In other words, it suggests to us that we may be able to fool others with our pious acts of holiness, but God cannot be fooled. God cannot be mocked, tricked, or hoodwinked into blessing us and healing us. We must be sincere and aligned with his practices and purposes.

God's promise for obedience to His way of fasting is revealed in verse 8:
"Then shall thy light break forth as the morning, and thine health shall spring forth speedily: and thy righteousness shall go before thee: the glory of the lord shall be thy reward."

Sometimes health comes when we shift our focus. We can get man's attention by lip-service, adherence to checklists, and busywork. This is obeisance. But only a true commitment to God's precepts can move us from obeisance to obedience. That's what gets God's attention.

When we abandon unproductive behaviours that give the appearance of obedience and begin to truly obey His plan, we can experience His healing.

"There is a way that *seemeth* right unto a man, but
the end thereof, are the ways of death."

Proverbs 16:25

DAY 21

Point 5. Ministry-Our Response to Miraculous Healing.
Gratitude for healing is a demonstration of thankfulness that is not necessarily audible, but is visible in one's living, one's giving, and the calling upon one's life. To show gratitude, those healed by Jesus followed Him, ministered unto Him, and labored in His service. A life of service is a more powerful testimony than words uttered before a crowd.

In fact, many times Christ bade those who were healed not to tell anyone. As a result of my study, I noted that Christ did not want the multitudes to see what He did and begin to worship Him prematurely, rather than worship the Father who had sent Him. That would have only served to intensify the anger of the religious zealots who were already against Him (Mark 9:31). Christ healed and raised people from the dead so that they might go on God's errands and glorify God.

This is a template for us. Our mission is to tell others about God's goodness. While it is a good thing to speak your witness, it is better to be a witness.

"Let your light so shine before men, that they may see your good works, and glorify your Father which is in heaven."

Matthew 5:15

DAY 22

The following chart summarizes the record of faith, humility, and importunity demonstrated by those who sought healing in the Bible. It also shows the resulting ministries of those who were healed. Their obedience is implied.

WOMAN WITH ILLNESS	DEMONSTRATION OF FAITH, HUMILITY, & IMPORTUNITY	EVIDENCE OF MINISTRY
Woman with the Alabaster Box Mark 14:3-9	She found the house where He had been invited to dinner, came there and began to wash and anoint Him…. Christ pronounced to her, "Thy faith has saved thee. Go and sin no more." Luke 7:50	By worshipping Him….In an act of worship and faith in His ability to save her, she anointed His feet with ointment after washing them with her tears and drying them with her hair. Mark 14:3-9
Women healed of evil spirits and infirmities Luke 8:2	They were healed. Luke 8:2	By ministering….They followed Him throughout every city and village and ministered unto Him with their substance; after the crucifixion, they prepared spices and brought them to the sepulcher. Luke 8:3; 24:1, 10
Jairus' daughter Mark 5: 35-43	Jairus was there waiting for Him (Jesus) to return. Jairus fell down at Jesus feet and asked Jesus to come to his house, even though other people thronged him (scolded him) for doing so. Luke 8:40-41	By living….She lived; and He charged them that no man should know it. Luke 8:56

"Many are the afflictions of the righeous, but the Lord delivereth him out of them all."

Psalm 34:19

WOMAN WITH ILLNESS	DEMONSTRATION OF FAITH, HUMILITY, & IMPORTUNITY	EVIDENCE OF MINISTRY
Gentile woman who had a daughter with unclean spirit or devil. Matthew 15:21-22	She followed Him into Tyre and Sidon, and fell at His feet. Jesus told her: "O woman, great is thy faith: be it unto thee even as thou wilt and her daughter was made whole from that very hour." Matthew 15:28	By living a new life….And He charged them that they should tell no man. Mark 7:36
Woman with a spirit of infirmity for 18 years Luke 13:11	She came to the synagogue where He was preaching on the Sabbath day. Jesus said to her, "Woman, thou art loosed." Luke 13:12	By glorifying God…Immediately she was made straight, and glorified God. Luke13:13
Woman with issue of blood Mark 5:27-34	When she heard of Jesus, she came in the press behind, and touched His garment. For she said, if I may but touch His clothes, I shall be made whole. Jesus told her, "Daughter, thy faith has made thee whole." Mark 5:28, 34	By going in peace, free from illness…She fell down before Him, to which He replied, "Go in peace and be whole of thy plague." Mark 5: 33-34
Mother-in-law with high fever Matthew 8:14	They went to the synagogue and told Jesus that Simon's mother-in-law lay sick. He took her by the hand and lifted her up and immediately the fever left her. Mark 1:29, 31	By ministering…She arose and ministered unto them. Matthew 8:15 Mark 1:31

"And I will restore unto you the years that the locusts hath eaten…"

Joel 2:25

MAN WITH ILLNESS	FAITH, HUMILITY, & IMPORTUNITY	EVIDENCE OF MINISTRY
Leper Mark 1:40	The leper was beseeching Him (Christ) and kneeling, saying: "If thou wilt, thou can make me clean. Mark 1:40-41 Jesus answered by saying, "I will; be thou clean."	In offerings…See thou say nothing to any man; but go thy way, shew thyself to the priest, and offer for thy cleansing those things which Moses commanded, for a testimony unto them. Mark 1:44
Blind Bartimeus, the beggar Mark 10:46	And when he heard it was Jesus of Nazareth, he began to cry out and say…Have mercy on me. And many charged him to hold his peace, but he cried more a great deal, Thou Son of David, have mercy upon me. Mark 10:47-48 Jesus replied to him, "Go thy way; thy faith has made thee whole." Mark 10:52	By following Jesus…Received his sight and followed Jesus in the way. Mark 10:52
Two Blind Men Matthew 9:28	According to thy faith, be it unto you…See that no man know it.	They spread Jesus' fame and brought someone else to be healed - a dumb man who was also possessed with a devil.
Centurion's servant sick with palsy and grievously tormented Matthew 8:5	I have not found so great faith, no not in Israel… Go thy way; and as thou hast believed, so be it done unto thee. Matthew 8:10,13	Servant was made whole, indicating that he continued to minister in his customary way (serving his nation and building synagogues- see Luke 7:5)

"Death and life are in the power of the tongue…"

Proverbs 18:21

MY OWN ILLNESS	DEMONSTRATION OF FAITH, HUMILITY, & IMPORTUNITY	EVIDENCE OF MINISTRY

"But I have prayed for you, that your faith should not fail; and when you have returned to Me, strengthen your brethren."

Luke 22:32

DAY 23

Why is there suffering on earth? Sometimes suffering happens to people who did nothing to bring it upon themselves. Other times, suffering can occur as a result of our life choices. If we indulge in a detrimental habit or activity, suffering may occur later as a natural effect of what we did.

If we smoke tobacco, our chances of contracting lung cancer in the future are greater. A physician, Dr. Anthony Espinet, came to our local church to conduct a health seminar. He mentioned that diabetes is an illness that we "buy at the store." You might be able to readily cite some exceptions to each of these generalizations, wherein heredity and other factors played a part. Please don't miss the point. I am not a physician and each set of circumstances is unique. However, some illnesses work on a cause and effect principle.

Take a moment today to think about your lifestyle choices. Make an inventory of the practices that are promoting your good health and which practices are capable of destroying your health. Do something wise that may improve your future.

One man I visited in the hospital had heard the health message (plant-based diet to combat high cholesterol, exercise to improve cardiovascular health, etc.) for 25 years. His family practiced these health principles. He scoffed at eating vegetables without meat being added to flavor them. He rationalized, "as long as I take my blood pressure medicine, my doctor says I can eat what I want to." Before his last bout at the hospital for surgery, the pre-op staff gave him a special diet. It was essentially a fast from solid foods. In addition, he was also instructed not to take his usual array of daily medications. On the morning of the surgery, when the nurse took his pre-op vitals, the man's blood pressure was normal! The surgery was successful. Convinced at last about the benefits of a healthy diet to combat high cholesterol, the man vowed that once he left the hospital this time, the first thing he was going to do was to see a nutritionist.

Unfortunately, the man developed other complications and he never left the hospital alive.

This story is not included to bring fear. It is a simple illustration of the fact that most of us make lifestyle changes in our lives too late for the changes to have a significant effect on our mortality, life expectancy, or quality of life.

"...as it is said, Today if ye will hear his
voice, harden not your hearts."

Hebrews 4:7

DAY 24

The last thing that someone wants to hear when they are suffering is, "God wants to build your character." A suffering person wants relief.

You may be suffering now—physically, mentally, or emotionally. However, if you can somehow find meaning in your suffering and fix your sights on something beyond the immediate, you can improve your chances of making it through the difficult situation. That was the philosophy that made Dr. Martin Luther King, Jr.'s 1963 "I Have a Dream" speech so powerful. Although Negroes in the southern United States of America were treated unfairly, King's philosophy gave them hope that there was equality and fulfillment to come in the future.

One of the most powerful books written in the last century was , "Man's Search for Meaning," which was written by Victor Frankl, MD. During the Holocaust, Dr. Frankl became a prisoner of war, was stripped of his station in life, and was tortured. He and fellow prisoners endured some of the most harsh treatment mankind has ever inflicted upon mankind. Yet, he was successful; he survived. He inspired fellow prisoners and lived to tell the story.

How did American Negroes endure? How did Victor Frankl survive? The answer to that question is, incidentally, the answer to your own query, "How will I make it through this ordeal?" The answer lies in finding meaning, either in your suffering, or in the life that awaits you on the other side of suffering.

Frankl's definition of despair is suffering without meaning. If you can find something to live for, you will improve the quality of life that you have, whether you are suffering or not.

Our Saviour, Jesus Christ, suffered scourging, even to death, so that we might live eternally. If you are suffering in this life, you can be certain of this: there will be no suffering in the life to come. Focus for a moment on the sacrifice that Christ endured during the Crucifixion. As you endure earthly suffering, you become acquainted with the experience of

Christ. Won't you thank Him for loving you enough to give you hope and meaning during your time of suffering? Can you thank Him for the gift of eternal life?

"We are troubled on every side, yet not distressed; we are perplexed, but not in despair; Persecuted, but not forsaken; cast down, but not destroyed; Always bearing about in the body the dying of the Lord Jesus, that the life also of Jesus might be made manifest in our body."

II Corinthians 4:8-10

DAY 25

About 2 decades ago, my best friend's father was hospitalized for surgery. He had myriad complications that were associated with uncontrolled high blood pressure and flagrant mismanagement of his diabetes. At lunchtime one day, I went to visit him at the local hospital.

"Mr. Johnson," the very young physician began. "Your chances are not good; the infection has spread more rapidly than we thought initially. It is now in your brain, and there's nothing we can do. I'm sorry." Mr. Johnson's large frame suddenly looked fragile, weaker than it had been just moments before. He cowered behind the crisp white sheets as he pulled them nervously to his chin.

His had been a big, looming figure. He was so large that he darkened rooms when he entered the doorway. Yet the mere words of the young physician delivered a TKO (Total Knockout) punch.

After she left, I somehow felt it was my responsibility to give Mr. Johnson hope. In recent years he had not been a church-goer. So I didn't want to preach to him. I knew that he was tremendously proud of his young grand children so I told him,

"Mr. Johnson, only God knows when your time is up. _He_ numbers your days, not man. So, Mr. Johnson, don't give up. Focus on living, rather than focus on dying. Find something to live for. Do you want to see your grandson grow up? He nodded, yes. Okay, then fix your mind on seeing your grandson playing in Little League, then in High School. Think of the traditions that your family enjoys. He nodded again. And then when God heals you and raises you up out of this room, give Him the glory by serving Him."

Mr. Johnson left the hospital that month. He got better and he lived several additional years—in fact long enough to see that grandson go to high school and to witness many more memorable family occasions. And he joined a men's Bible Study group and began to attend church. He died when it was his appointed time to do so—and not one minute

before. Best of all, as he continued day by day, I gathered the impression that he was living with his health challenges, as opposed to dying with them.

"Man that is born of a woman is of few days and full of trouble. He cometh forth like a flower, and is cut down: he fleeth also as a shadow, and continueth not…seeing his days are determined, the number of his months are with thee, thou hast appointed his bounds that he cannot pass."

Job 14:1,2, 5

THE RESPONSE TO MIRACULOUS HEALING IS MINISTRY AND SERVICE TO GOD.

Build up the Kingdom

Let your light so shine before men that they shall see your
good works and glorify your Father, which is in heaven.

Matthew 5:16

DAY 26

Think About It …

1. Have you ever been miraculously healed from an illness?

_____

_____

2. What role did faith, humility, obedience, or importunity play in your own healing?

a. _____

b. _____

c. _____

3. How have you shown gratitude for your healing?

a. _____

b. _____

4. In what ways have you ministered to others?

a. _____

b. _____

5. What is the role of modern-day medicine in today's world? How does it fit into God's plan for healing the sick?

_____

_____

"But the God of all grace, who hath called us unto his eternal
glory by Christ Jesus, after that ye have suffered a while,
make you perfect, stablish, strengthen, settle you."

I Peter 5:10

DAY 27

There are Five Traits that those who were healed by Christ shared. They are:

Faith ... Humility ... Importunity ... Obedience ... Ministry

Let's further examine these traits. The first trait that those who were healed shared is Faith. Faith puts us in touch with the will of God concerning us. By reading and hearing His word (the Bible) we learn His will for our lives and more about His ways. As we pray for the things that are in His will and will bring Him glory, we can be assured that, "He will supply all of our needs according to His riches in Glory"(Philippians 4:19).

Faith should give us the ability to accept whatever the outcomes are. Healing? Okay. No healing? Still okay. Our journey should lead us to an acceptance that He is Sovereign and that He is working all things for our good. Be assured.

"And we know that all things work together for good to them that love God, to them who are the called according to his purpose."

Romans 8:28

DAY 28

Here are some "Gems of Faith" regarding illness and healing. Place a check next to the statements that bring you comfort as you journey toward wellness.

Gems of Faith

☐ Beloved, I wish above all things that you will prosper and be in good health, even as thy soul prospers. III John 1:2

☐ Honor thy father and thy mother: that thy days may be long upon the land which the LORD thy God giveth thee, for this is the first commandment with promise. Exodus 20:12

☐ The days of our years are threescore years and ten; and if by reason of strength they be fourscore years, yet is their strength labour and sorrow; for it is soon cut off, and we fly away. Psalm 90:10

☐ Behold, happy is the man whom God corrects: therefore despise not thou the chastening of the Almighty; For he makes sore, and binds up: he wounds, and his hands make whole. Psalm 5:17-18

☐ And fear not them which kill the body, but are not able to kill the soul: but rather fear him which is able to destroy both soul and body in hell. Matthew 10:28

☐ In all this Job sinned not, nor charged God foolishly. Job 1:22

☐ But I have prayed for thee, that thy faith fail not: and when thou art converted, strengthen thy brethren. Luke 22:32

☐ For therein [in the gospel of Christ] is the righteousness of God revealed from faith to faith: as it is written, the just shall live by faith. Romans 1:17

* * *

The effectual, fervent prayer of a righteous
man [or woman] availeth much.

James 5:16

DAY 29

Not all treatment plans lead to recovery. How we manage our disappointment is key.

My father fought a valiant battle against the ravages caused by infection from surgery.

He was a sportsman and a Tennessee Sports Hall of Fame Coach. Daily, I encouraged him in sports terminology … telling him, "We're still in the game."

Or when there was progress, I would tell him, "It's only half-time and now we're up by two."

When my father died, I left his room, deflated.
At the time of his illness, one of my spiritual mentors was an associate pastor at his church. When I turned the corner after leaving the hospital suite, I saw her.

"We didn't win," I told her.
She said, "Oh, but we did. A Believer wins either way. If we are healed, we live on earth,we win. If we go to sleep in Jesus, we live again and we win. When we are in Christ, we are in a 'Win-Win.'"

I thought about it for a moment. She was right.

"For as the sufferings of Christ abound in us, so
our consolation also aboundeth by Christ."

II Corinthians 1:5

DAY 30

Humility. Humility puts us in touch with the suffering of our fellow man. More important, it puts us in touch with the suffering that Christ endured on our behalf. It puts us in the exact position necessary for God to start to bless us with His healing power.

Consider these pearls of wisdom concerning humility. Check the box next to the ones that resonate with you most.

☐ If my people, which are called by my name, shall humble themselves, and pray, and seek my face, and turn from their wicked ways; then will I hear from heaven, and will forgive their sin, and will heal their land. II Chronicles 7:14

☐ For as the sufferings of Christ abound in us, so our consolation also aboundeth by Christ. II Corinthians 1:5

☐ And whosoever shall exalt himself shall be abased; and he that shall humble himself shall be exalted. Matthew 23:12

☐ But he giveth more grace. Wherefore he saith, God resisteth the proud, but giveth grace unto the humble. James 4:6

☐ And thou shalt remember all the way which the LORD thy God led thee these forty years in the wilderness, to humble thee, and to prove thee, to know what was in thine heart, whether thou wouldest keep his commandments, or no. Deuteronomy 8:2

Humble yourselves therefore under the mighty hand
of God that He may exalt you in due time. Casting
all your care upon him; for he careth for you.

I Peter 5: 6-7

DAY 31

Importunity. Importunity is our search for healing, to leave no stone unturned in our quest for wholeness. Read all you can. Pray for direction. Pray to be led into the pathways of those who can help you. Seek the Lord. Keep your heart merry by enjoying all that life has to offer (i.e., music, art, movement, laughter, reading, movement activities.)

Select the Bible promises that speak to your petitions to God for healing:

☐ And shall not God avenge his own elect, which cry day and night unto Him, though He bear long with them? Luke 18:7

☐ Behold, the Lord's hand is not shortened, that it cannot save; neither his ear heavy, that it cannot hear: Isaiah 59:1

☐ And all things, whatsoever ye shall ask in prayer, believing, ye shall receive. Matthew 21:22

☐ If a son shall ask bread of any of you that is a father, will he give him a stone? Or if he ask a fish, will he for a fish give him a serpent? Or if he shall ask an egg, will he offer him a scorpion? If ye then, being evil, know how to give good gifts unto your children: how much more shall your heavenly Father give the Holy Spirit to them that ask him? Luke 11:11-13

☐ Behold, he that keepeth Israel shall neither slumber nor sleep. Psalm 121:4

☐ A merry heart doeth good like a medicine. Proverbs 17:22

There are two sides to the importunity lesson for us as Christians. When the requestor relentlessly begs for favor, the grantor must demonstrate the compassion of Christ and if possible, grant the request. Like Christ, we must be willing to look at our neighbor's condition and hear with our hearts, before we hear with our ears. We must fill some unspoken needs out of compassion, if we determine there is a need.

Perhaps someone in need has come to you for help. List the requests that you now have the power to fulfill.

"And all things, whatsoever ye shall ask in prayer, believing, ye shall receive."

Matthew 21:22

DAY 32

"One for you...one for me...one for you...one for me...," began the child in a popular TV advertisement some years ago. He was counting out small candies for himself and his friend. The little boy's candy count-out showed what it means to bestow blessings upon a friend.

As I think about John's blessing to his friend in Christ , who was known as Gaius, my mind wanders to the little boy who counted candies. John said to Gaius:

"Beloved, I wish above all things that thou mayest prosper and be in health, even as thy soul prospereth." (III John 1:2)

For years, I often wondered why John seemingly issued a *conditional* blessing for the health and prosperity of his friend. I pondered to myself, "Why didn't John unequivocally pronounce the blessing of good health upon his friend?" Why did John find it necessary to add, "***even as thy soul prospers***"? In my heart, I thought John's blessing was *almost* unfair, and not a *real* blessing at all. That was, until I realized the power of spiritual healthiness.

A man (or woman) is truly healthy when the spiritual being and the physical being operate in tandem. When this is the case, the person's countenance reflects the harmony of life style, life force, and life purpose. God is glorified by the person's words and deeds. When others see him or her, they see a reflection of ***God's best*** for mankind.

Consequently, it is a dangerous thing for a man to be physically healthy and spiritually sick. If he is physically strong, yet spiritually sick or weak, he will have the energy to run on errands of the Enemy (Satan) while having the strength of a healthy body that has been restored by God.

So, while you are taking medicines and treatments to heal the physical body, also reflect, pray, and seek alignment with God's purpose for

your life. This will strengthen your spiritual being and God will be glorified.

If you are ill, pray for your full recovery, which means the spiritual **and** the physical faculties, healing simultaneously, or at the same time.

"Beloved, I wish above all things that thou mayest prosper and be in health, even as thy soul prospereth."

III John 1:2

DAY 33

Obedience. Obedience is a responsibility, but it carries with it, a blessing. The blessing is the harmony that it fosters between man and his Creator. This is known as spiritual alignment. When you are walking in obedience, you want to do what pleases God. This is spiritual maturity. This is likely what it means to have a perfect heart toward Him.

When your heart is perfect toward Him, your thoughts and ways are like His. You no longer find pleasure in what displeases Him. You will have reached spiritual maturity. When your heart is perfect towards Him, you can watch Him work on your behalf. When you are sleeping, fatigued from treatment, often being made more ill by the treatment, itself—when your body is tired and your will is low, take no care, for God is a very present help in your time of trouble. The scripture reads, "God is our refuge and strength, a very present help in trouble" (Psalm 146:1).

Which of these texts resonate most within you?

☐ And all things, whatsoever ye shall ask in prayer, believing, ye shall receive. (Matthew 21:22)

☐ And in thy seed shall all the nations of the earth be blessed; because thou hast obeyed my voice. (Genesis 22:18)

☐ If they obey and serve him, they shall spend their days in prosperity, and their years in pleasures.(Job 36:11)

☐ And Samuel said, "Hath the Lord as great delight in burnt offerings and sacrifices, as in obeying the voice of the Lord? Behold to obey is better than sacrifice, and to hearken than the fat of rams." (I Samuel 15:22)

Many people marvel about the faithfulness of Daniel. I marvel that Daniel had an "excellent spirit." (Daniel 6:3). No doubt this came as a result of his relationship with God. Daniel's life is a testimony to this relationship. The outward signs of the inner relationship were his obedience and the decisions that he made, even regarding the food that he ate:

"At the end of the ten days [Daniel and his friends] looked healthier and better nourished than any of the young men who ate the royal food."(Daniel 1:15) NIV

By now you may be saying to yourself inwardly, I haven't always been obedient, so now that I need God's help, I am not eligible to receive it. No worries here. God has made provision for all who will fall short of the mark and disobey. It is found in the following text:

"And refused to obey, neither were mindful of thy wonders that thou didst among them; but hardened their necks, and in their rebellion appointed a captain to return to their bondage: but thou art a God ready to pardon, gracious and merciful, slow to anger, and of great kindness, and forsookest them not. (Nehemiah 9:17)"

Isn't that wonderful news that you can depend on God? Trust Him. Get some rest. In fact, all of your earthly physicians may be asleep this morning, but the Bible reassures us about the Great Physician: "Behold, he that keepeth Israel [us] shall neither slumber nor sleep" (Psalm 121:4).

Isn't it reassuring that nothing goes unnoticed on His watch. God is awake. Pray for a perfect heart toward Him.

"For the eyes of the LORD run to and fro throughout
the whole earth, to shew himself strong in the behalf
of them whose heart is perfect toward him."

II Chronicles 6:9

DAY 34

Ministry
List three ways that you can use what you learned during your personal journey to help others.

1. _____

2. _____

3. _____

You can gain spiritual wisdom by studying the Word of God. Through the scriptures, God has given me answers to my problems over and over again. Each time that I am Spiritually led, I am pleased, yet somewhat amazed how He guides me in ways in which "people of the world" do not believe, understand, or validate.

Think about a problem you may be facing. The problem can be physical, spiritual or emotional. Ask God to give you answers. As an act of faith, open the Bible to the location that God impresses upon you to read. While reading, you may become inspired to read from another book or chapter. Follow your inspiration. Keep reading until you understand your problem better.

When you have been healed, relieved of your burdens or enlightened, go on God's errands. Glorify Him in your walk, not only in your talk. The five traits that lead to wellness are the same that lead to salvation: Faith, Humility, Importunity, Obedience, and Ministry. That is why Christ could both heal sickness and save souls, simultaneously.

"Let your light shine before others, that they may see your good deeds and glorify your Father in heaven."

Matthew 5:16

CREATIVE HEALING

DAY 35

Creative Healing is good for:

Creating Psychological Distance between you and the problem.
It is effective in providing relief for the types of problems that are usually resolved in time (grief, loss, anxiety). Creative Healing helps in these situations because it separates you from the problem. This has the same effect as time.

Giving you a Temporary Diversion from your problem. Use Creative Healing to work on problems that are not life-threatening, when you are not in immediate danger. When you are endangered or when a loss of life or limb is at stake, a more immediate intervention is necessary. Don't be "penny wise and pound foolish."

Enabling you to enjoy the Balance of Your Life. From the moment we are born, we actually begin the process of dying. Disease, misfortune, and emotional issues can hasten and draw our attention to that process. Creative Healing can restore quality to your life and in doing so, you can begin living with your illness, rather than dying from it.

"And thou shalt remember all the way which the LORD thy
God led thee these forty years in the wilderness, to humble
thee, and to prove thee, to know what was in thine heart,
whether thou wouldest keep his commandments, or no."

Deuteronomy 8:2

DAY 36

What can you do while you are waiting for healing to occur?
Engage in Creative Healing

A Gallup Poll cited that 96% of all Americans believe in a Higher Power or Universal Spirit. People who meditate, reflect daily and trust in God attest to the benefits of the spiritual alignment that it brings.

In 2000, my mother had a knee replacement. As she reached a new milestone during her physical therapy session, she exclaimed, "Praise the Lord." The therapist remarked to her, "People who know God have an easier time [recovering from] with this surgery." During times of personal crisis, the belief that you do not face your problems alone promotes resolution and brings comfort. Even if you are not a Christian, you will benefit if you spend some time everyday:

. Thinking about your life and its purpose
. Counting your blessings
. Reflecting over the day's events
. Writing your feelings in a journal
. Giving thanks
. Planning for personal time and activities that you enjoy

In addition to these traditional meditation activities, take the challenge to medicate yourself through Creative Healing. Creative Healing is the use of the arts: reading (biblio), music, art, movement, and even laughter to promote well-being.

Movement allows the body to remain lithe and flexible over time[5]. Depending upon your fitness level and condition, select low-impact or high-impact activities. Walking is my favorite. On the island of Bermuda, there are some residents, well into their sixties, seventies, and eighties who enjoy a daily swim. Among their peers, these individuals demonstrate the most vitality, vigor, and stamina.

Like walking, sports and aerobic exercises are cathartic and expressive.

They can improve your sense of well-being by providing a worthwhile use of leisure time and keeping your body fit.

A walk on the beach, through the woods, on a nature trail[6], or in your own back yard garden can bring peace and repose. These activities can help you to strongly connect with the Creator. In times of wellness, many people do not think about God. But when sickness and despair fall upon human beings, the natural response is to seek help from God.

"The heavens declare the glory of God; and the firmament showeth his handywork."

Psalm 19:1

PARTICIPATING IN CREATIVE HEALING CAN PROVIDE AN AVENUE FOR DIVERSION.

DAY 37

Bibliotherapy. In a similar sense, reading books can provide a diversion from the life issues you may be facing. Recently I talked to a successful business manager. He recalled his high school experience to me as one that had been peppered with family troubles. These troubles were due to a parent who battled mental illness. The manager credited his own survival to a high school English teacher who provided books for him about far away places and exciting events. The books became the vehicle that provided solace and comfort for the young man. They rescued him from a shattered home environment. Reading caused the young man to be very well-read and educated beyond his formal education. It sparked his ambition to achieve. It kept him from becoming a victim of his environment. None of his classmates suspected the student's family difficulties. This was bibliotherapy at its best.

Like this young man, you too, may be facing tough issues. By selecting books with stimulating or interesting topics, you may be able to find a temporary solace. There is a strong possibility that you will return more invigorated, refreshed and thereby, better equipped to tackle your issues.

Bibliotherapy, according to Jacqueline Stanley in *Reading to Heal*, is the therapeutic use of books in the treatment of illnesses or personal problems (p.3).

She further states, "In Ancient Greece a plaque was placed over libraries stating: "A Place of Healing for the Soul" ... and by 1850, every major mental hospital had a library. (p.4)

The benefits of bibliotherapy are many. In a personal crisis, reading subject-specific material can give you a proper understanding of the related social, emotional or spiritual issues. Through reading and processing your thoughts, you simulate a counseling relationship with the author. As the reader, you can gain awareness about the subject, acquire knowledge, experience attitudinal shifts and, ultimately, make behavior changes. As the reader, you obtain treatment at your own pace.

Whenever you need aid and comfort, the books are there. Your reading is personal; you can include others in your treatment or choose not to.

If you have a physical illness or medical condition, reading can also give you more information about your illness and help you to make informed decisions about your treatment and care. Once you are healed, reading can help you to maintain your wellness.

Be sure to include among your reading stories from "The Greatest Book Ever Written," the Holy Bible.

"The fear of the LORD is the beginning of knowledge:
but fools despise wisdom and instruction.….Be not wise
in thine own eyes: fear the Lord, and depart from evil. It
shall be health to thy navel, and marrow to thy bones."
Proverbs 1: 7 ; Proverbs 3:7-8

"Thy word is a lamp unto my feet and a light unto my path."
Psalm 119:105

DAY 38

Music Therapy. Another form of creative healing is music therapy. We often hear the adage, "Music soothes the savage beast." You may recall the Biblical story of how David saved his own life from the hand of the crazed Saul by strumming his harp. After David strummed the harp, King Saul put down the javelin and David was unharmed.

I recall a similar personal healing experience with music, specifically, Chopin's Prelude in E minor. In the midst of a personal emotional crisis, I played this selection on piano. As I played it over and again, it seemed that the melody and its massaging harmonies bathed my emotions and soothed my restlessness like a cooling brook covers parched rocks after a long drought. The tension and release of the prelude's chromatic harmonies worked through my distress as skilled hands can manipulate throbbing muscles. Looking back over that experience, I marvel at what the Poet of the Piano (Frederic Chopin) was able to achieve through 25 measures and an anacrusis.[7]

Department stores routinely use music therapy. After sampling factors such as their typical customer's age and economic/social status, merchants select and pipe in music that will motivate the customer to stay in the store longer. The longer they stay in the store, of course, the more they buy.

"And it came to pass, when the evil spirit from God was upon Saul, that David took an harp and played it with his hand: so Saul was refreshed, and was well, and the evil spirit departed from him."

I Samuel 16:23

DAY 39

Laughter Therapy. Your brain receives a similar release when you laugh. Laughter therapy is the most newly documented form of creative healing. At this writing, a few authors have written on the subject, conducted workshops, and consulted with organizations about how to use humor to reduce stress in the workplace. These writers say that laughter increases oxygen levels, releases endorphins from the brain cells, and strengthens the immune system. The strongest case for laughter therapy among other forms of creative healing is that laughter has an immediate effect on one's mood.

It can break the chain of despair instantly. Other forms of creative healing are more process-oriented and if the user is not careful, the thoughts of despair can co-exist while the art form is being expressed, practiced, performed, or engaged in.

"A merry heart maketh a cheerful countenance: but
by sorrow of the heart the spirit is broken."

Proverbs 15:12-14

DAY 40

Art Therapy. Because an artist's canvas or other medium is a reflection of the mind's eye, participation in artistic activity can assist in a release of suppressed feelings or can allow an individual to express the content of the soul.

Samuels and Lane reinforce this idea in their book, ***Creative Healing***:
"An artist is a way of being, a way of seeing. An artist looks at light, at shadows. An artist looks deeply into each moment (p. 107)."

With this in mind, consider the artistic imagery David conveyed in II Samuel 23:4 when he wrote:

"He is like light flooding the earth at dawn on a cloudless day; He is like the sun that fills the sky after the rain; He makes every blade of grass sparkle like a diamond in the field and sprout from the ground."
(The Clear Word).

Whether through art, laughter, music, movement, or reading, creative therapy can play a part in helping you to achieve and maintain a sense of personal balance and wellness. Use the following tips to explore creative therapy.

Tips:
- Visit a website on Laughter Therapy
- Visit the church, hall, or synagogue of your choice on a regular basis
- Unleash the artist inside you!
- Play a musical instrument, alone or in a group. If you do not play an instrument, compile a personal play list and listen to it regularly.
- Choose a mode of artistic expression. Make it a part of your schedule as you add more preferred activities to your schedule.
- Engage in the art form and journal about your results. Use the enclosed "Schedule and Reflect" form for your journaling. Request these forms at info@breakco.com.

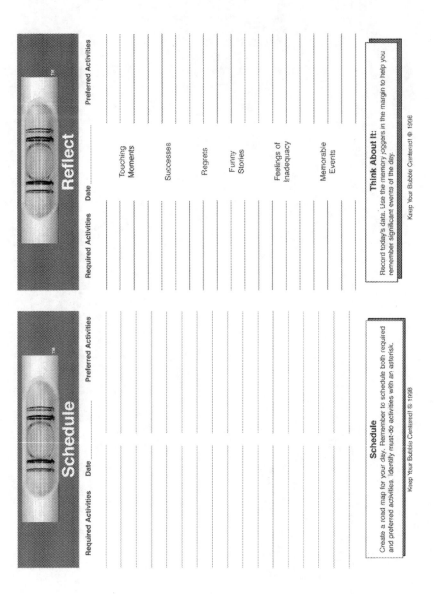

Schedule

Date _____

Required Activities | Preferred Activities

Think About It:
Record today's data. Use the memory joggers in the margin to help you remember significant events of the day.

Keep Your Bubble Centered! © 1998

Touching Moments

Successes

Regrets

Funny Stories

Feelings of Inadequacy

Memorable Events

Reflect

Date _____

Required Activities | Preferred Activities

Schedule
Create a road map for your day. Remember to schedule both required and preferred activities. Identify must-do activities with an asterisk.

Keep Your Bubble Centered! © 1998

"O give thanks unto the LORD; for he is good;
for his mercy endureth for ever."

I Chronicles 16:34

Endnotes

[1] The evidence that Jesus practiced pharmacology is as follows:
When he had thus spoken, he spat on the ground, and made clay of the spittle, and He anointed the eyes of the blind man with the clay, And said unto him, Go, wash in the pool of Siloam. He went his way therefore, and washed, and came seeing. John 9:6

[2] The Two Great Commandments, are these:
Jesus said unto him, Thou shalt love the Lord thy God with all thy heart, and with all thy soul, and with all thy mind. This is the first and great commandment. And the second is like unto it, Thou shalt love thy neighbour as thyself. On these two commandments hang all the law and the prophets. Matthew 22: 37-40

[3] Importunity is shameless persistence. This definition was given by Joel Olsteen on a television evangelistic program. The Bible gives this example:
"And he said unto them, Which of you shall have a friend, and shall go unto him at midnight, and say unto him, Friend, lend me three loaves; For a friend of mine in his journey is come to me, and I have nothing to set before him? And he from within shall answer and say, Trouble me not: the door is now shut, and my children are with me in bed; I cannot rise and give thee. I say unto you, Though he will not rise and give him, because he is his friend, yet because of his importunity he will rise and give him as many as he needeth. (Luke 11:5)."

[4] After Christ had been crucified, buried, and had resurrected, Paul and the disciples continued to teach about Christ. They were imprisoned and

brought before the high priest. When defending their practice to teach the multitudes about Christ, Paul and the other disciples echoed, "We ought to obey God rather than men."

[5] The section, "Creative Healing: is a reprint from *Keep Your Bubble Centered: How to Achieve Personal Balance.* Adapted and included by permission of publisher: BreakThrough Communications. Available from www.breakco.com

[6] In this printing, sports was included to create the section on movement. It was contributed by Dr. Leslie Holder, based on his personal experience. As part of his own personal therapeutics, Leslie enjoys nature, particularly spending time on the beach (early morning), or in the woods and vigorous exercise such as swimming in the ocean and playing basketball (even at age 65).

[7] The anacrusis in music is also called the "pick-up beat." The pick-up beat occurs before the first full measure of a song. It is the result of an unfinished measure at the end of the song which, in effect, allows the song to be played over and over without pause between the last measure and the first measure. The anacrusis or "pick-up" provides a rhythmic accent to the first beat of the first measure, making it sound stronger and more emphatic.

REFERENCES

Text References

Agatson, Arthur, M.D. 2003. *The South Beach Diet.* New York: Random House.

Blanco, Ph.D., Jack J. 1994. *The Clear Word: An Expanded Paraphrase of the Bible.* Hagerstown, MD: Review and Herald Publishers.

Bostick, Alan. 1999. "The Art of Healing: Vanderbilt Hospital treat patients with music, poetry and art," *The Tennessean*, Sunday, July 25, page 1K.

Lachkar, Ph.D., Joan. 1998, 2004. *The Many Faces of Abuse.* Maryland: Rowman & Littlefield Publishers, Inc.

Lockyear, Herbert. 1958. *All the Men of the Bible.* Grand Rapids: Zondervan.

Pearsall, Paul, Ph.D. 1987. *SuperImmunity: Master Your Emotions & Improve Your Health.* New York: McGraw-Hill.

Smith, Constance Ridley. 2001. *"Keep Your Bubble Centered: How to Achieve Personal Balance."* Nashville: Breakthrough Communications.

Stanley, Jacqueline. 1999. *Reading to Heal: How to Use Bibliotherapy to Improve Your Life.* Boston: Element Books.

The Holy Bible Authorized King James Version (KJV), Crown Reference Edition, 1985. Nashville: Holman Bible Publishers.

Vine, W.E., Unger, Merrill F. and William White, Jr. 1985. *Vine's Expository Dictionary of the Bible.* Nashville: Thomas Nelson, Inc.

Online References
Bibletab.com, Online Concordance Containing one reference from the New American Bible http://www.biblegateway.com King James Version

http://www.biblegateway.com, King James Version

Blue Letter Bible. "Gospel of Luke 13 - (KJV - King James Version)." Blue Letter Bible. 1996-2012. 17 Mar 2012. http://www.blueletterbible.org/Bible.cfm?b=Luk&c=13&t=KJV

Blue Letter Bible. "Gospel of Mark 7 - (KJV - King James Version)." Blue Letter Bible. 1996-2012. 17 Mar 2012. http://www.blueletterbible.org/Bible.cfm?b=Mar&c=7&t=KJV

Audio
Simpson, India Arie. 2009. "Testimony Volume 2, Love and Politics," *The Cure.* Universal Republic Records.

Televised
The back cover description was inspired by a televised interview with Bishop Joseph Walker of the Mount Zion Baptist Church of Nashville, Tennessee. Bishop Walker's concept on "40 days" in the Bible was significantly enlarged upon and adapted for this publication.